·GROWING UP IN·
Ancient China
KEN TEAGUE

Illustrated by
RICHARD HOOK

Troll Associates

Library of Congress Cataloging-in-Publication Data

Teague, Ken, (date)
  Growing up in ancient China / by Ken Teague; illustrated by
Richard Hook.
    p.   cm.
  Includes index.
  Summary: Describes daily life in ancient China, discussing life in
the country, life in the city, schools, festivals, and other
aspects.
  ISBN 0-8167-2715-5 (lib. bdg.)   ISBN 0-8167-2716-3 (pbk.)
  1. China—Social life and customs—To 221 B.C.—Juvenile
literature. [1. China—Social life and customs—To 221 B.C.]
I. Hook, Richard, ill. II. Title.
DS741.65.T43   1993
931'.01—dc20   91-14879

Published by Troll Associates

© 1994 Eagle Books

Design by James Marks
Edited by Kate Woodhouse

Printed in the U.S.A.

10 9 8 7 6 5 4 3

Contents

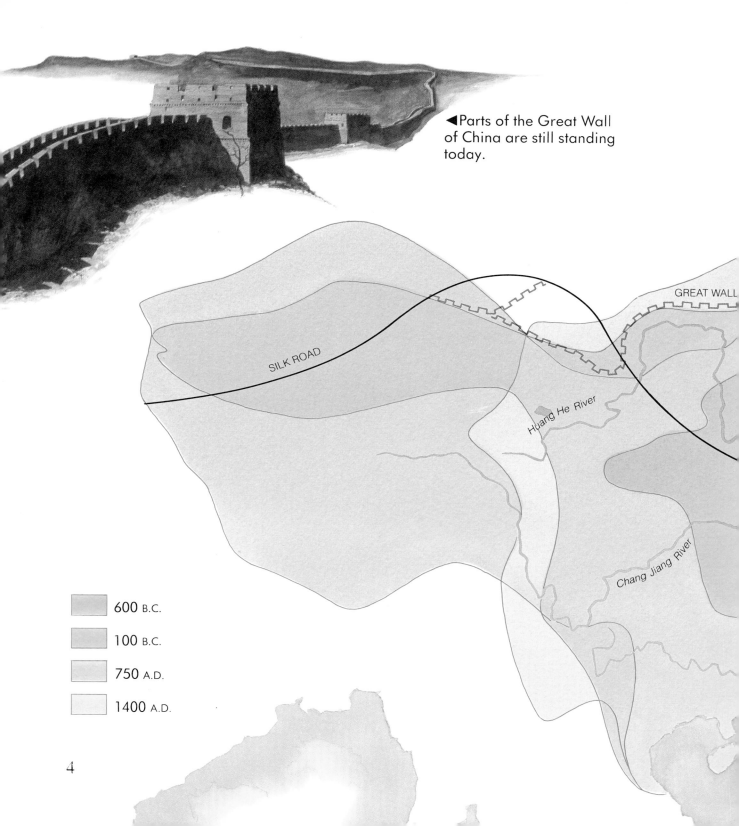

◄Parts of the Great Wall of China are still standing today.

GREAT WALL

SILK ROAD

Huang He River

Chang Jiang River

	600 B.C.
	100 B.C.
	750 A.D.
	1400 A.D.

4

Who were the ancient Chinese?

The ancient Chinese were originally hunters and fishers. They lived along the Huang He and Chang Jiang rivers, in northern and central China, about 5000 B.C. They settled in these fertile regions and became farmers. They grew millet and rice, raised pigs and goats, and made fine pottery.

The Chinese civilization grew and thrived over thousands of years. China developed its own culture of arts, philosophy, and science. In some ways the life of people in the villages of China today is not very different from that of their ancestors 2,000 years ago.

◄This map shows the boundaries of China at different stages in its history. In 600 B.C. the Zhou dynasty ruled an unsettled and divided country, but by 100 B.C. the Han dynasty controlled a strongly united China. Under the Tang dynasty in 750 A.D. China expanded greatly, but by 1400 it had lost some of this land. The Great Wall was built over two thousand years ago to keep out the warlike people to the north.

▼This bronze vase was made in about the 14th century B.C. It is 10 inches (25 centimeters) high.

EAST CHINA SEA

SOUTH CHINA SEA

ing

Birth and birthdays

Birthdays were times of presents. Before a birth, the mother's parents would send her flowers, food, sweets, and clothes for the baby. When a boy was born, he was given a piece of jade, and a bow was hung outside his family's doorway. A girl was given a curved roof tile, and a handkerchief was hung outside. More presents were given when the baby was 100 days old. A popular gift was a padlock to "lock" the baby into a long and healthy life.

▼Everyone believed that ghosts could harm people, especially children. Parents dressed their children in clothes decorated with designs and charms to protect them against evil spirits.

The Feast of Lanterns celebrated the births of the previous year. The family hung a special lantern in the ancestral hall or the village temple to announce a birth formally, and the baby was introduced to his many ancestors and living relatives. Afterward, there would be a Banquet of Lanterns feast.

Daily life

Chinese children were brought up to be gentle, friendly, polite, and obedient. They were taught to respect their elders, not to answer back, and not to sit when someone older was standing. Children were never beaten, but were told stories of ghosts such as "Big-eyes Yang" or "Liu the Barbarian."

Everyone in the household got up at dawn. An ancient book lists the duties of the children of officials. Once they were up, had washed their hands, rinsed their mouths, combed their hair, and dressed, the children had to gather up their pillows and mats and put them out to air. They had to sprinkle the floors of the rooms and courtyard with water and sweep them out. Then they went to their parents to ask if they were well, to take them water for washing, and to bring any food they needed.

▼A popular game was kicking a shuttlecock. Walking on stilts and playing marbles were also favorites.

Once these tasks had been done, the children were free to play. The younger ones played with animal rag dolls. Older children played with clay figures, musical instruments, masks, puzzles, or any other toys they might have bought from the toy peddler.

◄Kites were made from silk and paper on a bamboo frame in the shape of fish, birds, or butterflies. Some had bamboo pipes which made a noise when they were flying.

9

Dinner time

Dinner time was not a family occasion in ancient China. Men and boys over seven were fed first. Afterward the women and children under seven ate together. Babies were nursed by their mothers until they were about two, or until they had learned to use their hands for eating. People in the countryside ate at dawn, midday, and sunset. In the cities, stalls sold food at any time. Small figures made from soybeans, corn-flour cakes, or candied fruit were popular.

▼ Poor people lived mostly on a diet of rice, cabbage, and a little pork and bean curd. Their cooking utensils were roughly made. Salt was important to their diet, and the government controlled its production and sale.

▼The Chinese served food in small pieces so that they could eat it with chopsticks or spoons. They never used knives for eating. Small children quickly learned to use their chopsticks and to hold their bowl near their mouth to avoid dropping food.

Richer people had a great variety of food. It could be boiled, steamed in bamboo containers, fried in a shallow frying pan called a wok, or sometimes roasted. Cups, plates, and dishes were mostly made of wood and pottery.

The ancient Chinese were the first tea drinkers. They also drank honey, ginger, and fruit juices. They drew water from rivers, canals, lakes, and wells, but they never drank it on its own. In winter they cut ice from the rivers and lakes, and stored it in earth mounds for use in the summer.

Getting dressed

During the summer, small children often wore only an apron tied at the neck and waist. By the time they were three or four, they dressed much like adults. They might wear a robe or a tunic worn over trousers. Children from wealthy families wore leather shoes or silk slippers. Poor people wore wooden clogs or straw sandals. In winter, people relied on clothes rather than heating to keep warm. Everyone wore thick, quilted coats and several layers of clothes.

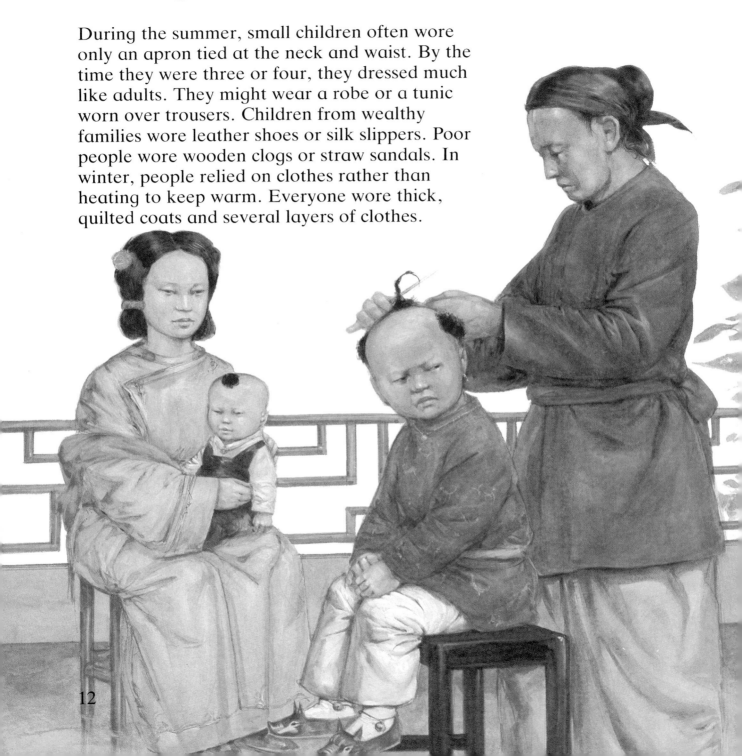

▼Hair cutting was an important event in ancient China. People were proud of their children's black hair. They often tied it with lucky red ribbons.

Decorations on clothes were seen as protection against evil spirits. Sons were thought of as especially important, because they would grow up to worship their ancestors and have more sons. So boys often wore clothes in the lucky colors of red and pink, perhaps embroidered with lucky animals. Children wore hats, collars, and shoes with designs of tigers, dogs, or pigs to scare away evil spirits.

Charms were also important. A boy might wear a plain metal ring like a dog collar to fool the spirits into thinking he was a dog. Earrings, necklaces, and anklets were worn as protection, as were colored threads fastened to clothes.

13

Inside a Chinese house

Some Chinese homes were rectangular. Others were square with courtyards inside. But all were built out of the same materials: wood, bamboo, brick, and tile. Most country houses had a courtyard, which was used as a working area, and where grain was threshed and dried on mats. Separate food-storage rooms were built on stilts to protect the grain from rats and damp. Vegetables were also grown in the courtyard, hedged off by a bamboo fence.

In the cities, 10 or 12 families often lived together in multi-story houses, with the ground floor used as a shop or workshop. Both adults and children slept on mats made from rushes or padded cotton, with wooden headrests, rather than pillows. The rooms were furnished with low tables, chairs, stools, and cupboards, all made of bamboo or black wood. Bamboo mats or animal skins covered the floors in poorer houses, while richer people had woolen carpets.

►Most houses had upturned corners on the roofs to keep away demons, because the Chinese believed demons traveled in straight lines.

On special occasions people would bring out any small antiques, flowers, and vases they owned to decorate their rooms.

14

Life in the country

Most people in ancient China were farmers. Even the youngest children helped on the farm. They would look after their work animal—a buffalo—by taking it to water and feeding it. Sometimes they would guide the buffalo when their father was plowing. Both boys and girls helped grind the rice for cooking. They also helped feed the animals, and older children took grain and vegetables to market in wheelbarrows. The main crops were rice in the south and center of China, and wheat in the north.

▼The summer months were the busiest, when farmers worked during all daylight hours. Children took food to their fathers at midday and helped in whatever way they could.

During the rice-growing season, children helped to transplant the seedlings, and hoe and weed them as they grew. Some of the flooded rice fields were also stocked with fish to eat. Once the rice was ripe, the fields were guarded by children with clappers to frighten away the birds. The farmers also slept in the fields when rice and vegetables were ripening to stop thieves. After harvest, the family gathered the rice straw and used it for thatch, mats, or sandals.

17

Life in the city

City life was lively and busy. The big cities had wide main streets with a maze of narrow alleys behind them. Along the main streets were open-fronted shops selling food, clothes, jewelry, books—almost anything you could want. Children sold food and candy from trays.

The emperors of China ruled from walled cities within larger cities. Members of the court, nobles, and foreign merchants also lived in the walled cities.

Trade was very important in ancient China. From the first century A.D., a famous trading route called the "Silk Road" stretched from China to the Mediterranean in Europe. Many Chinese inventions, such as paper making, and Chinese produce, such as silk and apricots, reached Europe along this and other overland routes. From the early 16th century, European ships sailed to China to trade. Chinese tea became popular in many parts of Europe and Asia.

▶Sometimes you might see musicians, jugglers, and other performers on the streets. Children and adults went to teahouses. Marco Polo, an Italian merchant who traveled to China in the 13th century, wrote fascinating stories about what he saw.

Town and country crafts

Children often took up the crafts practiced by their parents and started helping them when they were quite young. The range of Chinese crafts was enormous. In the cities, a family might own a small shop and make kites, puppets, or lacquered furniture. Some craftsmen, such as clog makers, worked in the streets or marketplace.

Most craftsmen were organized into groups called guilds. Each guild had a feast day, when the craftsmen hired musicians and dancers.

▼Weaving and embroidering cotton and silk were important crafts in the country. It was usually women who did this, although in the towns, men and boys also sewed in special workshops, making goods for the market.

The weavers' guild festival was one of the most important as so many people were weavers. It was held on the seventh day of the seventh moon, and all the children put on new clothes.

Some of the most skilled craftsmen made fine things for the emperor's court and the nobles. They made plates, bowls, and vases from porcelain, which they decorated beautifully. Most workshops produced simpler goods made from bamboo, wood, and earthenware.

Women in some parts of the country kept silkworms, an ancient and important craft. The children helped by gathering the thousands of mulberry leaves needed to feed the silkworms.

Going to school

Education was important in ancient China. Boys usually went to school at the age of seven or, if their parents were rich, they had a private tutor. In some cities the richest children went to special schools between the ages of 7 and 13, where they learned to write 20 Chinese characters a day. Girls were not usually sent to school. They learned to spin, weave, and embroider, and they helped their mothers at home.

Most farmers could not read or write, yet they valued education. If there was spare time from jobs in the house or on the farm, children were encouraged to practice copying characters with a brush and ink. In some villages there were winter schools. The pupils would recite together from books.

▶These children are learning Chinese calligraphy, or writing. It was a great art, because there were thousands of symbols, each representing a different idea. Chinese writing has hardly changed over 2,000 years.

Education and learning were made easier by the invention of paper making and printing in China more than 1,000 years ago. Books were easily available, so many people were able to study.

Children who were good scholars were sent to district schools and then possibly to college. A scholar who passed the examination to become a government official brought wealth and honor to his family.

Festivals and ceremonies

There were many festivals and ceremonies in ancient China. One of the most important celebrations was the New Year festival. It was also important to worship at family tombs, because ancestor worship was part of a child's religious training.

Funerals were important times for children: they were a kind of celebration that all the relatives attended. There was drumming and chanting, with fireworks to scare away the evil spirits. Paper copies of the dead person's house, clothes, and food were burned, to provide the soul with its needs in the next world.

The New Year festival was held about the end of January or early February. People hung new images of the gods over their doorway, and a special dish of red beans was offered to the guardian spirits of the house. Families gathered to celebrate New Year's Day and the following three days in their own homes. A few days later, the Feast of Lanterns gave everyone a chance to welcome spring with music and dancing.

►This family is honoring some of its ancestors. Tablets of wood were carved and painted with the name and birthday of an ancestor. People offered food, lit lamps, and burned incense before the tablets.

24

Travel and transport

China is an enormous country, and its people used many different methods of travel and transport. Water transport was particularly important. Some of the larger towns were linked by canals big enough to take sea-going boats. There were barges and bigger boats called *junks* that sailed along the rivers and canals and traded at the towns they passed. When the canals of the north froze in winter, the boats were fitted with special skis and poled along.

▼ The wheelbarrow was invented by the ancient Chinese. Their wheelbarrows had one or two wheels. Some were pulled with a rope at the front, and a wheelbarrow might even have a sail to help it on its way. This wheelbarrow is being used to transport people.

Boatmen and their families lived on their boats. Babies had bamboo floats tied to them until they learned to swim! As soon as they were old enough, children helped their parents on the boat.

Carts were used by country people to carry produce and people. The carts were pulled by oxen, donkeys, or horses. Rich men traveled on horseback, while women and children were carried in sedan chairs. Government officials had light, two-wheeled carriages pulled by one horse.

Getting married

In ancient China, when a boy was 20 and a girl was 15, they were ready to be married. The boy was now considered an adult and was allowed to worship his ancestors and to have sons to continue the family.

Marriages were arranged after a fortuneteller had declared that the couple were suited to each other. The dead ancestors and living relatives of the bride and groom were also consulted through prayer, and a suitable date for the wedding was set. The groom's family gave presents of jewelry and clothing to the bride's family, as thanks for bringing her up well. When she was engaged, the girl would pin up her hair with long pins to show that she was to be married.

The wedding was a big celebration. The bride was dressed in red clothes for good luck. The couple were tied together with a red thread and drank from the same cup to show their unity. The woman was now a member of her husband's family.

Over the centuries, China has gone through many changes. But no other culture in history has survived as long.

►The bride was carried to the groom's house for the wedding ceremony in a closed cart or sedan chair to avoid evil influences, and to show that her position in society had now changed.

28